# MUD ON THEIR WHEELS

the *Life-Story* of

VERN AND LOIS ELLIS

by

Betty M. Hockett

GEORGE FOX PRESS
P.O. BOX 44 • NEWBERG, OREGON 97132

To
JEFF
whose mother-in-law is happy
to call him "son."

**MUD ON THEIR WHEELS**

The LIFE-STORY of Vern and Lois Ellis

© 1988 George Fox Press
Library of Congress Catalog Card Number: 88-81703
ISBN: 0-943701-14-7

*Cover by Jannelle Loewen*

*Litho in U.S.A. by The Barclay Press, Newberg, Oregon*

# CONTENTS

1. The Miracle Well ....................... 1
2. No Time Wasted ....................... 9
3. Stuck in the Mud ...................... 17
4. Busy Days and Sleepless Nights ......... 23
5. One Big Happy Family ................. 31
6. A-E-I-O .............................. 39
7. Eight Dead Goats ..................... 45
8. The Appreciation Party ................ 53
9. Name That Tune ...................... 61
10. Remember When? ..................... 71

*Vern and Lois Ellis*

# Chapter 1

# THE MIRACLE WELL

"We must have a well here at Rough Rock or we'll have to move the mission," said missionary John Cline in 1952. "Would it be possible for Vern Ellis to come and drill a well?"

Vern already knew about this problem at the Friends mission located on the Navajo Indian Reservation in Arizona. "They've tried drilling for water before," he explained to his wife, Lois. "The hole turned out to be dry."

"You've had experience with well drilling," Lois replied. "If our church here at Springbank will give you time off, you'd better go to Rough Rock and see what you can do."

The congregation at the Springbank, Nebraska, Friends Church gladly agreed to give their pastor time to help at the mission. On February 17 he set out for Arizona, driving a big truck loaded with equipment for drilling the well.

As soon as Vern arrived John Cline explained, "This spot up here on the hill is where the Lord directed us to drill a few months ago. We can't understand why the drillers couldn't find any water."

"How deep did they go?" asked Vern.

"They drilled as far as their machine could go—190 feet," John replied. "The well at the government school here goes down 1,268 feet. We don't have nearly enough money to make a well that deep."

"Well, let's see what happens this time," said Vern as he started the motor on the drilling machine.

The machine began to whir and clank. Vern prayed as he watched the long cable going down, down, down. "God, this is your mission. Please make this try for water successful." He knew that people in several states were also praying.

The machine rattled and shook, but the bit went no farther. "It's hit a layer of rock!" Vern shouted to John. "We can't go any farther down."

The men discussed what to do. They didn't want to give up yet. "Let's try blasting out the rock with dynamite," Vern suggested.

One blast of dynamite didn't help. They prepared to do it a second time.

*Will this be successful?* Vern wondered.

\* \* \*

Vern Ellis waited for the dust and rock to settle from the blast. He looked out over the community of Rough Rock. The Arizona desert sprawled out yellow and brown and red in front of the hill. Black Mountain rose behind him.

Several hogans showed up amid the scattered piñion and juniper trees. These six-sided log-and-dirt houses were almost the same color as their brown surroundings. The Trading Post and a few other buildings stood in a nearby ravine. Off in the distance a flock of sheep grazed while their Navajo herder wandered along behind.

*This land is beautiful!* Vern thought. *Those huge reddish-brown rock formations out there are beauty created by God!*

He thought about the Navajo Indians who lived in this southwest part of the United States. That day he began to feel a love for them. *They need to hear about God's love*, he thought.

Vern wished his wife, Lois, and their children could have come along. He knew Keith and Joyce and Eva would enjoy an adventure like this. *Patricia would, too, except she's pretty little yet*, he thought to himself.

As soon as the dust settled, Vern and John ran to the well. There, they discovered water!

"Praise the Lord! We've hit water!" Vern exclaimed.

"How deep did you have to go?" John asked.

"Just 207 feet! I'll drill down a few more feet, though, to make sure the well will have plenty of water," Vern answered with a big smile on his face.

"This is definitely an answer to prayer!" said John.

When some of the government officials heard about the well they said, "It can't be! That's solid rock up there!"

"It's our miracle well!" John replied.

Vern added, "The Bible tells us how God brought water out of rock for the children of Israel. Now He's done it again!"

\* \* \*

Vern soon went back home to Springbank. "Those Navajos are wonderful people," he told Lois. "I wonder if someday God will call us to be missionaries at Rough Rock."

"Maybe so," Lois replied. "I don't imagine that would be for a long, long time, though."

During the next three years Vern made several more trips to Rough Rock to help with other special projects. His love and concern for the Navajos grew each time he went. The Ellis family grew also, with the birth of a daughter named Sandra.

In June 1955 the Friends mission board met in Denver, Colorado. Vern went to the meeting. While there he heard, "John and Marjorie Cline will soon be leaving Rough Rock. Vern, we feel you and Lois are the ones to go in their place."

"I'll have to talk to Lois," Vern replied, and rushed to find the nearest phone.

He told Lois what the board members had said. She felt as surprised as he did. "Of course God has been talking to me about this for a long time," Vern reminded his wife.

"We hadn't thought we would have opportunity to go this soon," she replied.

They prayed together on the telephone. When they had finished, Vern said, "I believe it's the thing for us to do."

"I do, too," Lois agreed from the other end of the line.

Vern hurried back to tell the mission board, "We'll go!"

\* \* \*

One night a few weeks later, Vern's loud whistle sounded throughout the parsonage at Springbank, Nebraska.

"Hey!" shouted 13-year-old Keith. "Dad wants us to meet together! That's what his special whistle always means."

"Come on, Patricia!" coaxed eight-year-old Eva. The three-year-old scrambled to join the family circle.

Lois sat in the rocking chair with baby Sandra asleep on her lap. Joyce, 12 years old, sat cross-legged on the floor.

"What would you think if we moved to Rough Rock?" Vern asked.

"That'd be exciting!" said Keith immediately.

"I think it sounds like fun," said Eva.

The Ellis family always worked well together. Right away they all did their part to help get ready for the big move. The church people assisted, too. In a few weeks they all said goodbye.

"It's hard to leave these wonderful people," said Lois.

"Yes," Vern agreed. "I've enjoyed being their pastor, but God has called us to be missionaries."

"It's like that time He spoke to us when we lived on the farm," Lois added. "We loved being farmers, but we knew God wanted us to prepare for full-time Christian service." They remembered how God had helped them attend Friends Bible College in Haviland, Kansas. They knew He would help them now.

Then they started on the long, tiresome trip from Nebraska to Arizona. They stopped in Colorado to borrow a large brown army tent. "We can live in this until we build a house," Lois said.

A few miles out of Shiprock, New Mexico, they turned off the paved road onto a narrow dirt road. Up over the Lukachukai mountains they went. Down on the other side they bounced over holes and humps on the desert trail. They lurched through the big dry ditches called *washes*.

"When it rains hard," Vern explained, "these washes will run full of water." They would soon know all about that!

At last they saw the landmark Vern had described. The big silver water tower sat high on the rocky hill above the community of Rough Rock.

Lois looked around eagerly. *This is our new home*, she thought. *What will it be like?*

# Chapter 2

# NO TIME WASTED

"I have a sick baby. He needs to be taken to the hospital right away. Can you take us?" asked the Navajo man who stood in front of Vern Ellis.

"Yes, I can do that," Vern replied quickly. He helped the man and the sick baby into the car and started off for the hospital at Ganado, seventy miles away.

When he got back home Vern said to Lois, "The baby would have died if we hadn't gotten him to the hospital."

"We've only been here 24 hours so far," she replied. "We sure haven't wasted any time getting into the routine of mission work."

Later that first week at Rough Rock a Navajo woman and her new baby came to the Ellis tent. "I've just come home from the hospital," she explained. "I live up on Black Mountain, but none of my family know I'm ready to go home. Anyway, they don't have a way to come get me."

Vern and Lois made room in their big tent for the two visitors. They stayed several days before the Ellises decided they should be the ones to take the woman and her baby home.

"How long did it take you to get down off the mountain?" Vern asked.

"Not long," she replied.

Vern quit working on the house at five o'clock that afternoon. Lois filled the teakettle with water and put it on the gas stove. "I'll leave the burner on low while we're gone," she said. "We'll be back soon. The water will be hot by that time, and I'll be able to get supper right away."

They started up the mountain. The farther they drove, the worse the road became. On and on they went! *We'll surely be there before long*, Vern thought. He had not yet learned the road, this being their first time on the mountain.

It got dark, but they kept going. Finally, they came to the top of the mountain and started down the other side. *I didn't dream we'd be gone this long*, thought Lois. *My teakettle has surely boiled dry by now!*

Suddenly the Navajo woman pointed at a tent set back in the trees. "Some of my relatives live there. I can stay with them tonight and go on home tomorrow."

Vern and Lois helped her to the tent before they started back down the mountain. By this time Lois really began to worry about the teakettle. "It may even have started to burn," she said.

They hadn't gone far when they discovered that rocks had cut into one tire. They hurriedly changed tires. Thoughts of the burning teakettle filled Lois's mind. *The whole tent may be in flames by the time we get back!* she thought.

At nine o'clock the Ellises returned to the tent. "At least the tent is okay," said Lois as she rushed inside. "The teakettle has boiled dry, but praise the Lord it didn't burn!"

\* \* \*

Vern and Lois spent the next few weeks getting acquainted with the area around Black Mountain. "Rough Rock is almost in the center of this huge Navajo reservation," Vern explained.

"Is it true that the Navajos are the largest tribe of Indians in the United States?" asked Eva.

"That's right," Vern replied. "There are over sixteen million acres on the Navajo reservation." He pointed to the map. "The Navajos are spread out over 25,000 square miles. Mostly they're in northeast Arizona. Some, though, live in southern Utah and western New Mexico. Almost all of them have goats and a few horses as well as their sheep. Some keep cattle, too."

"I already know the Navajos live in family groups called camps," said Keith.

"I like the beautiful rugs and saddle blankets the women weave from their hand-spun wool," said Eva.

"They sell them to earn money," Lois explained.

The Ellises quickly discovered their mail arrived only three times a week. Even then, they had to drive on 35 miles of bad roads to get it at the post office at Chinle. They could also see a doctor at Chinle, although Ganado had the hospital.

They soon learned the way to Farmington and Gallup, New Mexico. Vern went there to buy building supplies and repairs for the vehicles. They found out the Rough Rock Trading Post sold groceries as well as most of the other things they would need. "That's where the Navajos buy their supplies, too," said Lois.

Vern and Lois continued the Bible class John and Marjorie Cline had started for the children who attended the government school. Twenty-five boys and girls came to the mission for an hour every Monday afternoon. Lois used flannelgraph figures to illustrate the Bible story she told in English. Vern helped the Navajo children learn choruses. The boys and girls worked hard to remember their Bible memory verses.

Vern and Lois spent some time every day studying the Navajo language. "It's one of the most difficult languages in the world," Lois wrote to her parents. "The words are like a brick wall between us and the Indians. Of course, the children who go to school learn English there."

In the middle of October the Ellis family moved out of the sandy-floored army tent into their new house. "It isn't finished yet," Lois said, "but it's going to be a fine modern home."

*   *   *

One day that fall Vern learned of a fight.

"This group of young fellows started drinking pretty heavy," the trader explained. "They can't buy liquor here at the Trading Post, but they got it somewhere. As usually happens, a fight broke out. I called the police, but before they showed up one young man ran away." The trader pointed south. "He went into his hogan over there and shot himself!"

"His two brothers come to our Bible class on Monday afternoons," said Vern. "We'd better find out where his mother lives and go visit her. She's been attending our Sunday services."

After he told Lois, Vern said, "It has been the Navajo custom to leave the hogan in which someone died. Occasionally they will burn it. They believe that evil spirits stay around after death. The Navajos are extremely fearful of evil spirits."

"Why do they believe that way?" asked Eva.

"Even though the Navajos live in the United States just as we do, certain experiences have a different meaning to them," Vern explained. "Their customs and ways of doing things aren't the same as ours. That's why we want them to know of God's love. He can forgive them and give them freedom from the superstitions that frighten them so badly."

"The Navajos are religious, but many don't worship God the Creator," added Lois. "They worship things He has created, like the sun, moon, and fire."

Vern and Lois went to visit the sad mother. They bent over to enter the six-sided hogan through the only door. The Navajo woman motioned for them to sit on a pile of sheep skins. A red-hot half-barrel stove standing in the center warmed the small space. The black stove pipe pointed straight up through the hole in the top of the hogan. A tiny strip of light shone through the narrow open space around the stove pipe. Cold air blew in through there, too.

"My husband died last year," the mother told them as best she could in English. "Before long, my cabin caught fire. Now my boy is dead, and that hogan will be burned."

"We want to pray with you," said Vern gently. After he prayed he gave her some Navajo gospel records and a tiny phonograph she could work by hand. "We pray that God will help you," he said.

\* \* \*

"It won't be long until Christmas," said Lois in November. "I'd like for us to do something special for the Navajos."

She quickly wrote letters to friends in Colorado and Nebraska. The letters said, "You can help us! We want to give a special gift to everyone who comes to our Christmas service."

Packages and money began to arrive. The mission, the Trading Post, and the school worked together on the community Christmas service.

As many people as could, crowded into the church on December 21. Others stood outside to listen through the open windows. "I believe there must be 350 people here," Vern whispered to Lois.

The dusky-skinned men wore blue jeans. Big felt hats sat atop their shiny black hair. The women had on full-flowing gathered skirts of colors such as bright blue and purple. Their pretty velveteen or plush blouses were hidden beneath colorful blankets closely wrapped around them. Some had carefully drawn their hair back and tied it with a length of handspun yarn.

After the program everyone received a sack, a cup of coffee, and a sweet roll. The children couldn't wait to see the treasures inside their sacks.

"Peppermint candy!" exclaimed one.

"A little car and some marbles," shouted one boy happily.

"I got jacks and barrettes," said an older girl.

Men found key chains and combs in their sacks. The women smiled as they pulled out plaques, combs, needles, pins, and buttons.

"Even the babies have something," reported an excited older sister. "See? Rattles!"

The Cracker Jack, oranges, apples, candy, and gum pleased the sack holders, too.

On Christmas day Vern and Lois directed a service at the church. Afterward, each Navajo received a gift of clothes. The children had toys, also.

Later Lois wrote to her friends in Colorado and Nebraska, "The Navajos appreciate the clothing you sent. It gets quite cold here so warm clothes are essential. I wish you could have seen the happy faces and heard the big thank-you's. We appreciate all who have made this possible!"

\* \* \*

After a few months Vern and Lois told the mission board, "We need a school here at Rough Rock Friends Mission where the Indian children can live as they attend classes. A school would be a ministry in the community. We would like to begin this fall."

Vern attended meetings of the Indian Tribal Council and explained the ideas for the school. The council gave a permit for the mission to go ahead.

The missionaries planned the school building. "It will be big enough for twenty Navajo children to live in and study in," they said.

During that summer of 1956 Lois and an interpreter visited many of the family camps. "We're going to have a school. Will you sign up your children for our school?" she asked.

Friends came from many places to help with the school building. Others wrote to say, "We're praying for you."

Lois answered those letters. "We couldn't keep going if it weren't for your prayers. That's what holds us up!"

One morning a man hurried onto the building site. "Can you take a sick lady to the doctor?" he asked.

Vern looked at Lois. "I don't think I can take that much time off from working on the school building today," he said.

"I could take her," Lois replied. She loaded the sick lady into the pickup and headed for Chinle.

Late that afternoon Vern put his hammer down. He looked in the direction of the mission house. "Lois should have been home by now!" he said to Keith. "I wonder what's happened to her?"

*Rough Rock area with the mission buildings in the foreground and Black Mountain behind*

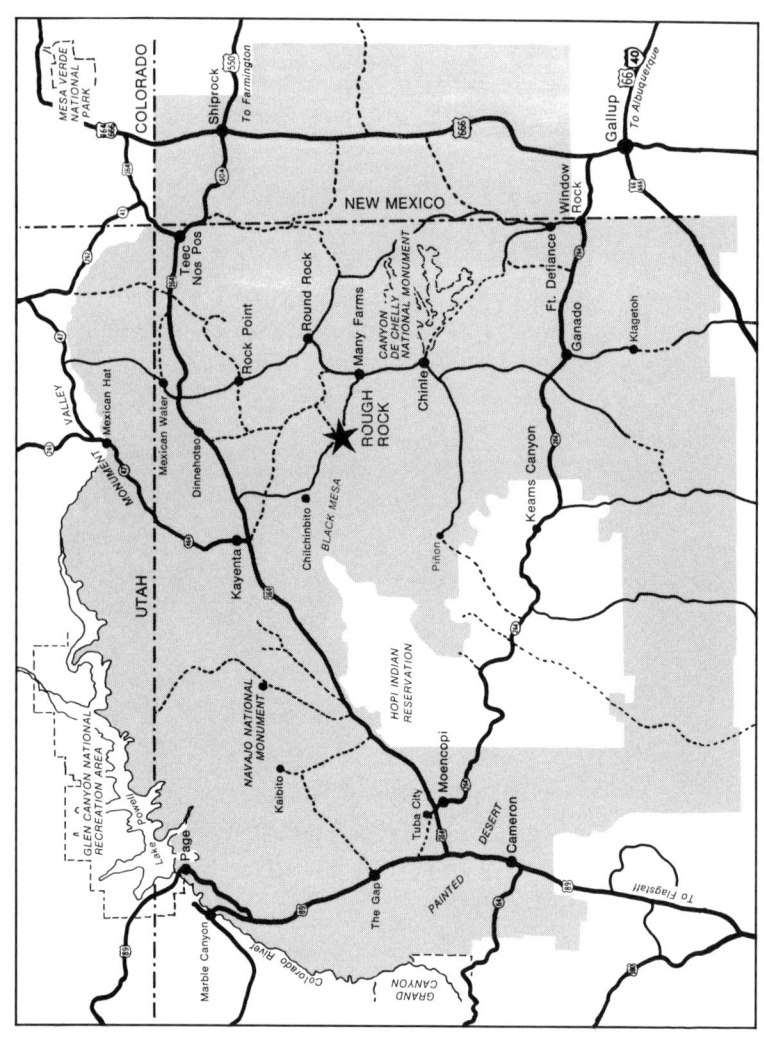

# Chapter 3

# STUCK IN THE MUD

"Daddy, maybe Mama's stuck in the mud somewhere," Keith suggested.

Vern looked out across the desert. "Those clouds have been awfully dark over that way all afternoon. It's probably rained hard between here and Chinle. Come on, Keith, we'll get the old truck started and see if we can find her."

"Okay, I'm coming!" Keith climbed down the ladder. "Look! Here's the shovel. We took it out of the pickup to use on the building. Mama doesn't have anything to dig out with!"

They ran to the big mission truck and hopped in. Vern pressed the starter. After a few rounds the motor charged into action.

"I suppose they're back from the doctor by now. I know where Lois would have to go to take the sick lady home." Vern steered the truck over the bumpy wagon roads. They bounced along for several miles before they came to where it had rained.

"The road looks like a river!" said Keith. Water sprayed high around the truck as it bounced along. The daylight slowly disappeared. Keith looked from side to side, hoping to see his mother. Vern watched the tracks ahead.

In the last light of day, Vern spotted what he had been looking for. "There she is!" he shouted. "And just as we thought—the pickup's mired down in the mud."

They got there as fast as they could through the water. Vern and Keith jumped out and grabbed their shovels. Lois stood in mud nearly up to her knees. Rain dripped off her skirt. Her light brown hair hung straight down like wet strings.

"Am I glad to see you!" she said with a tired voice. "I did everything I knew to get out of here. Even after I put the chains on the tires, they wouldn't budge. It seems hopeless!"

"Keith, you work on that side," said Vern quickly. "I'll try clearing it out over here."

The gummy mud stuck to their shovels. It soon made their shoes twice as big as usual. As fast as they shoveled the mud out, more water filled the ruts.

"It seems like we're getting in deeper," Keith said after a while.

Vern nodded. "We need to go back up the road a ways and make a dam. If we can force the water off to one side, we'll have a better chance of digging the wheels out of this sticky stuff."

It took two hours of hard work. "Finally we're making some progress," Vern said. "Let's start the motor and try it another time."

Lois held tightly to the steering wheel. Vern and Keith pushed. The pickup slipped and slid, then jerked forward inch by inch. Finally it struggled out of the mud hole!

Both vehicles drove into the yard of the mission house at midnight. Joyce and Eva ran outside to meet them. "Poor Mama!" they exclaimed.

"Well, it was something that had to be done," said Lois as she took off her shoes. "We're here to help the Navajos any way we can."

"Come eat the supper we've fixed for you!" said Joyce.

The midnight supper tasted good. "Thank you, girls," said Lois.

\* \* \*

The workers finished the school building in time for school that fall. Mary Gafford came from Penrose, Colorado, to be the teacher. Roy and Frances Johnston arrived from Nebraska to help.

Thirteen children in grades three to eight settled into the routine of school at the mission. Vern and Lois sent a prayer request to their friends: "Pray for the children that they may give their hearts to Jesus and then win others to Him." Before long, eight boys and girls prayed for God to forgive their sins.

Vern and Lois helped at the school. They also kept busy doing things for other Navajos. By this time the Indians knew they could trust the Ellises. "They care about all of us, whether we go to church or not," they said.

They felt welcome at the mission house, day or night. After being invited in they would sit in the comfortable chair next to the door. Polite Navajos always waited a bit before saying why they had come. As they sat quietly the guests entertained themselves. They liked the fascinating chain-and-ring puzzle Lois left on the table beside the chair.

Sometimes the Indians came just to rest and visit away from the hot sun. Others needed aspirin or to use the telephone. Some Navajo adults who couldn't read or write asked Lois to write letters for them. She learned that many of them had not been to school. "For a long time there were only a few schools out on the reservation," someone said.

"I'm glad to do this," said Lois. "It helps me get better acquainted with the families."

Many times the Navajos who came on business brought family members with them. They all crowded into the living room. Vern and Lois took time to visit with everyone. They had opportunities to tell them about God's love and how He sent Jesus to give His life for them. If guests happened to be there at mealtime, Lois graciously invited them to eat with the family.

Every day Vern and Lois prayed, "Please help us present the Gospel in a meaningful way. We want the Navajos to accept You as their Savior." They loved the Navajos. They laughed with them and cried with them.

"The Navajos have become our brothers and sisters!" Lois said.

Vern and Lois spent lots of time visiting in the homes of the Navajos, too. They read the Bible, sang hymns, and prayed with the families they visited. Often the Indians said, "That's the first time we've ever heard that Bible story."

Sometimes they left records and record players so the Indians could hear the Scriptures in their own language over and over again.

"I'm so glad we have these records from Gospel Recordings and Gospel Broadcasters," said Vern.

\* \* \*

"I must make a trip into Gallup," said Vern one morning. "A man from here was killed in an accident in Wyoming. I'll meet the train and bring his body back. We'll have the funeral tomorrow morning. It'll be the first funeral ever held in this community."

At eight o'clock the next morning, thirty Navajos gathered at the church. They listened attentively as Vern preached in English and a Navajo interpreted.

Members of the family placed a new outfit of clothes in the casket with the dead man. "This is according to custom," someone explained. They also put in a handful of silver coins.

"He will need all of these things in the hereafter," his mother said. Then she put the rest of his clothes and his saddle in the ground with the casket. "This is the way we've always done."

Later Vern told Lois, "We'll trust that the message and the song helped her."

\* \* \*

Lois kept a big box filled with aspirin and other kinds of medicines. "We never know what we might need when we go visiting," she told her family.

One day as she visited in a hogan, the Navajo mother said, "I think my little boy has a fever. Will you take his temperature?"

Lois took the thermometer out of her box. "Does he know how to hold this in his mouth?" she asked.

"Oh yes!" replied the mother confidently.

Lois stuck the thermometer under the little boy's tongue.

CRUNCH!

"Oh my!" Lois exclaimed. "He bit it in half!" She quickly grabbed a Kleenex from her pocket and wiped out his mouth. "I don't know how much of the thermometer's mercury he might have swallowed. I'm going to call the doctor!"

She drove to the Trading Post and explained the situation to the doctor over the phone.

"Just give him bread and milk," the doctor advised.

She bought a loaf of bread and a quart of milk to take back to the Indian home. She told the mother what to do.

"I never did know if he had a fever or not," Lois said later, after the little boy recovered with no bad effects.

\* \* \*

Vern made sure he never left home without a shovel. He also took a good supply of matches. The uncertain condition of the roads always made any outing away from Rough Rock a hazard.

He made many trips to the doctor and hospital. Vern never complained about the long drives. "Babies about to be born and people dangerously ill with burns or high fevers need quick attention," he said.

Vern woke up at 2:30 one winter morning to the noise of a pickup stopping in front of the mission house. The pickup door slammed. The knock came next. He crawled out of bed and hurried to see who it could be. There stood a young woman.

"I have to get to the hospital at Ganado. I talked a neighbor into bringing me this far. My baby will be born soon. Can you take me?"

"Yes!" Vern answered. He dressed quickly and helped the young woman into his pickup. Her little boy and an aunt went along.

Globs of snow that looked like giant marshmallows decorated the juniper trees. The reservation lay quiet under its white blanket.

Vern drove cautiously. They made it safely to Chinle.

Soon after that the icy road began the climb along the ridge. Suddenly the pickup skidded. Vern twisted the steering wheel to try to keep the pickup on the road. Even so, it began to slide sideways.

Then, all at once, it stopped sliding as it went into the ditch and slowly turned over on its side.

Lois and Raymond, the toddler Vern and Roy brought home from the hospital

# Chapter 4

# BUSY DAYS AND SLEEPLESS NIGHTS

"Are you hurt?" Vern asked anxiously.

"No!" said the young woman.

"No!" said the aunt.

"No!" said the little boy in his high-pitched voice.

"Good!" Vern answered. "I'll go for help. You stay here in the pickup and keep as warm as you can!"

He shoved the door open and climbed out. For the next eight miles he didn't see anyone else. Then, at last, he found a ride. The driver helped him locate a doctor and a nurse.

On the way back to the pickup they met another vehicle. It had just picked up the three stranded passengers. "We're doing okay!" they said. The doctor and nurse got in with them, and they went off toward the hospital.

Later, men from a mission in Ganado helped Vern tip the pickup back up on the road. "Looks like the only damage is this cracked side-glass," one of the men said.

The next day Vern heard good news: "The young woman has given birth to a healthy baby boy!"

\* \* \*

Now and then Vern and Roy Johnston drove into Gallup to buy building supplies. On the way home they would stop at the Ganado hospital to see if anyone from Rough Rock needed a ride home.

One day the nurses were especially happy to see the men. "Raymond has been ready to go home for the last few days," they said. "Nobody could come for him. We know it's late in the day, but can you take him?"

Vern looked at the happy toddler. "Sure, we'll take him. He'll have to stay at our house tonight, but that'll be okay."

They arrived at the mission about ten o'clock. "Look who we've brought!" said Vern, holding Raymond up to Lois.

She looked surprised. "My, it's been a long time since we've had a baby to take care of! But we'll manage somehow. He has a bottle, and I can fix him a bed."

Before long Raymond slept soundly on a pile of soft blankets. Lois tiptoed in to look at him several times during the night. In the morning she cooked oatmeal for his breakfast. Then she and

Vern took him to his own home around the mountain.

"It's Raymond!" his mother and grandmother exclaimed.

"How did you take care of him?"

"Did he sleep?"

"What did you feed him?"

Lois laughed and handed Raymond over to his mother. "He's been as good as could be," she said. "He was perfectly content at our house!"

\* \* \*

Vern and Lois and their children felt close to one another. They sang together, went on picnics, played games, and teased each other. Even if they had been up all night helping someone, the parents were up early. They cheerfully said "Good morning!" and helped the children get ready for the day. They showed them the importance of being on time. Vern and Lois encouraged their children. "Can't never did anything!" they said.

Keith hauled rock and gravel for new buildings. He willingly worked on other parts of the construction, too. The girls helped cook for the work crews. They did the washing and ironing. Now and then they pounded nails or helped dig ditches.

All the children taught Sunday school classes. They led the singing at services and gladly assisted out on the playground.

The family read the Bible and prayed together every day. Vern and Lois freely told their children about the joys and the frustrations of their work. The children heard their parents pray many hours for the Navajos.

Other people came to help at the mission. Some, such as Mary Gafford and Diane Hutson, stayed for a long time. Many came for just a short while. Often, though, the Ellises were by themselves.

They sometimes had their own church service. All seven took turns leading the singing, sharing Scripture, praying, and giving testimonies. If one child felt angry at another, that feeling disappeared as the family prayed. "Those were outstanding experiences," Keith said many years later.

The children received some of their schooling through a course that came in the mail. Each morning, as soon as the breakfast dishes were finished, they started on their lessons for that day. They worked until they completed those pages, even if it meant working after supper. Lois stayed close to help when they needed her.

The mission school offered grades three to eight. After it opened the Ellis children went to classes there. Later, one by one, they went away to high school at Haviland, Kansas. Each time Vern and Lois cried a little bit and said, "We know it's the best thing for you. We'll sure miss you, though!" They prayed for their absent children every morning.

Sometimes the Navajos wondered, "What would a Christian family do?" They looked at the Ellis family to find out.

* * *

"I think we should give out the used clothes only after church on Sunday," Lois suggested. "That way the Navajos will get the Gospel as well as the clothes."

Vern agreed. "I've noticed that people who come for clothes during the week don't always come back for Sunday service."

The plan worked well. "The clothes are really a blessing," said Lois. She wrote to thank people in many states: "The Navajos really appreciate the clothes you have sent. The mothers especially are happy for the baby blankets, nighties, and diapers."

Lois visited in a home where a new baby had been born. She found the tiny baby wrapped in a flour sack. He lay on the floor in the warmth of the stove.

"I have something for you," said Lois to the mother. She handed her a blue flannel blanket and a bundle of baby clothes. The young Navajo woman smiled and said, "Thank you," over and over. She looked at the clothes one piece at a time. Her eyes filled with tears. "Who did this for me?" she asked.

"People who love you," replied Lois.

"I can hardly believe that anyone would care enough about me to do this wonderful thing!"

Making the Navajos happy with special gifts brought joy to Vern and Lois. Praying with their brown-skinned brothers and sisters gave them even more happiness.

One spring morning two young women came to the door of the mission house. "We told our camps this morning that we are going to be Christians," one of them explained.

"Now we want to know more about the Bible and how to be saved," said the other.

Vern and Lois invited them inside. They spent a long time helping the young women understand what the Bible said about being saved. "You must tell God you are sorry for your sins," said Vern.

"And pray for God to forgive you," Lois added.

Before long the four of them knelt beside the couch to pray. The young women both asked God to forgive them.

"Please bless these dear ones," Vern prayed. "Give them special courage and strength to live as You want them to live every day."

Vern and Lois kept up their busy round of activities every week. Their planned schedule looked like this: Sunday—Sunday school, afternoon worship service, Christian Endeavor, preaching in the evening; Monday—Bible classes for the children from the government school; Tuesday evening—4-H sewing classes for the mission school girls; Wednesday evening—language classes for the Navajos; Thursday evening—prayer meeting.

Christmas programs and caroling occupied December days. Daily vacation Bible school and camp meetings became a regular part of summer.

"I don't think any day ends like you thought it would," said one visitor. "There's always the unusual and unexpected."

Vern chuckled and replied, "The saying here is, *If it's boring at Rough Rock, just wait 15 minutes and something will happen!*"

One year Vern wrote on his report to the mission board: "This year I flew 10,000 miles in the mission plane and drove the vehicles 18,000 miles."

"My, aren't we glad for the airplane," said Lois as she read the report. "I'm so thankful you got your pilot's license while we were farmers."

"I'm pleased that Horace Mott loaned the plane to us. It sure has saved a lot of miles of travel on these bumpy roads."

"Being able to fly people to the hospital has saved several lives, too," Lois reminded her husband. "The thirty-minute trip by plane is a lot quicker than the two-and-a-half hours to Ganado by road."

Vern could quickly drive the short distance to the dirt airstrip where he kept the cream-colored and red plane. He often flew over the reservation to hunt for someone who hadn't returned home on time. Sometimes he helped by dropping shovels to people stranded in sand or mud. He found it handy to haul supplies by plane rather than trucking them into Rough Rock.

One day an elderly Navajo woman flew home to Rough Rock with Vern. "Did you enjoy looking out over the reservation from the air?" he asked.

"I didn't see anything," she answered. "I covered my head with my blanket!"

Vern always carefully checked the wind as he got ready to land at Rough Rock. If it seemed too blowy, he flew low over the mission house. Lois knew that meant she should hurry out to the airstrip. She had learned how to grab the strut of the plane as it landed. "The extra weight on the windside will be enough to keep this light-weight plane from flipping," Vern had explained.

One afternoon as Lois sat visiting with a guest, she heard the plane. "That's Vern!" she said. "We'll need to go out to the airstrip and help him land."

Lois, the visitor, and the girls piled into the car. On the way they met Keith. They stopped so he could go along, too.

"Now as we come up to the top of this little hill we go real slow," said Lois. "The road comes onto the runway. We don't want to run into the plane."

They came to the top of the hill.

"Where's the plane?" Keith wanted to know.

Then they all saw it at the same time, halfway down the landing strip.

"It's upside down!" screamed Eva. Her hands flew to her face in horror.

The car shot toward the upside-down plane!

## Chapter 5

# ONE BIG HAPPY FAMILY

Lois stopped the car beside the plane. Vern yelled as he crawled out, "I'm okay! Don't worry!"

Lois and the others couldn't get out fast enough. They rushed to Vern, nearly knocking him over.

"What happened, Daddy?" the children demanded.

"Well, after I buzzed the house, I decided it was okay to go ahead and land. While I taxied along a strong gust of wind caught the plane and flipped it over!" Vern smoothed his hair. "Come on, kids, you can help me look to see how much the plane is damaged."

Lois sighed with relief. "I'll drive back to the Trading Post. The trader and any other men standing around can come help put the plane back on its wheels."

After Vern checked the plane from propeller to tail, he said, "It's going to need some fixing. I think, though, it'll fly okay as far as Gallup. I know some mechanics there who can work on it."

A few days later he flew the damaged plane safely to the city for repairs. The little plane, blue and white thereafter, remained as an important part of the mission work for several more years.

\* \* \*

"I feel like God wants me to go talk to Amos and Marie Redhair," a Navajo woman told Vern.

"I'll be happy to take you there on my way home," he offered.

The next Sunday this woman brought Amos and Marie to church with her. Marie's brother and sister came, too. "We talked and prayed for God's forgiveness last night," they told Vern and Lois. "We want everyone to know that we've decided to follow God's way."

After the service Vern and Lois prayed with Amos and Marie Redhair. They talked to them about what it meant to be a Christian.

"I grew up here on the reservation," Amos explained. "While I was a boy I herded sheep and cared for the horses. My mother drank the juice of the peyote cactus. She would become drugged and then have visions. I learned to use it, too."

"I often was drugged with the cactus juice, also," said Marie. "When Amos and I were very young, my parents arranged for us to be married. But we've had a happy marriage."

"And now you have two children," said Lois.

*Amos and Marie Redhair, Navajo pastors for many years*

"In the meantime, I've been sick with tuberculosis for a long time. I heard about Jesus while I was in the hospital," Marie said.

Amos and Marie became regular attenders at mission services. They went to the camp meetings, too. "We should get rid of our peyote," they said one day.

Amos later testified, "Before I was saved I always drank wine or whiskey. All my life I tried to be great, but I never was. Now God is great in my life. I always will be true to the Lord. I want to worship and serve Him all the time. I am happy to follow Jesus!"

Amos used every spare minute to study his Bible. He and Marie soon became faithful workers at the Rough Rock Friends Mission.

\* \* \*

"Vern Ellis can fix anything," said the Navajos to one another.

Vern enjoyed being a "fix-it" man. His workshop gave him a place where he could tell people that Jesus wanted to be their Savior. Sometimes he reminded, "None of us will live forever. We need to make sure our soul is ready to meet the Lord." It wasn't unusual for Vern and a Navajo man to kneel down to pray there in the shop.

He didn't get flustered when a whole line of pickups waited for his help all at once. "I'll just help everyone in turn," he said calmly.

Vern's welding machine came in handy. He used it to build stoves for Navajo homes. He welded barrels to keep the precious water from leaking out through holes or cracks.

He took time to build looms so the women could weave their lovely designs into rugs and blankets.

Sometimes he asked himself, *Is this important?* Quickly he would answer, *Yes, it is! It's important to the Navajos. So, it's important for me to take time for this project so I can minister to them.*

\* \* \*

Vern and Lois moved into the apartment in the school building. "We'll be parents to the children in our school this year," they said. "We'll be one big happy family."

They woke up every morning to the sound of sleepy voices murmuring from both ends of the school building. After breakfast everyone had prayer and Bible reading together. Then the boys and girls flew into their work. Some washed and dried dishes. Others swept the floors or carried out the trash as someone else raised the flag.

"Many hands make light work," Lois told Ruth Cammack. She and her husband, Albert, had come from Oregon to help at the school.

"I've never seen a bunch of kids wash dishes any faster," Ruth replied.

The children also helped with supper. They did their own washing and ironing, too. Vern and Lois planned special events to help break the monotony of school life. Trips to the Navajo Tribal Fair at Window Rock, going to ball games, shopping at the Trading Post, and regular Saturday picnics made everyone happy.

Vern built a little car—big enough for several passengers. Although it had no motor, it had a regular steering wheel. "Our chitty," said the children. They took turns riding while others pushed it up the hill. Coming down brought squeals and screams of delight.

Vern also supplied the children with unicycles. "Better ride these in the gym," Vern warned. "The goat-head stickers out on the road will puncture the tires."

He showed the boys the proper way to use the shop tools and how to do leathercraft. Lois helped the girls with sewing and knitting. They both taught Navajo reading classes. Evenings were free for play. Just before bedtime, Vern read to the boys in their room while Lois read to the girls in theirs.

"The Ellises handle the children well," said a visitor. "They provide a good family life." Someone else remarked, "It's easy to see that the children love them. They are obedient and well-behaved and so happy."

"The boys and girls need to be loved, taught, and corrected just as if they were our own," said Lois. "It's a privilege to work with them. We're especially happy to help them pray to be saved from their sins."

Lois wrote many letters. "It's important to thank people who send money and gifts to the mission," she said. "I also want to keep folks informed about what's going on here."

She and Vern kept careful account of mission money. *That money comes from people's tithes and offerings*, they thought. *We must be careful how we spend it. We'll buy necessary materials, not just frivolous things.*

Friends who sent money said, "We're glad to give because we know our dollars go for the Lord's work at Rough Rock."

One morning Vern and Lois stepped out onto the back porch. The sun barely shone over the east edge of the reservation. Sounds of Indian chanting drifted in from faraway camps.

Vern shook his head sadly. "There's still so much superstition and sorrow among our Navajos. If only they worshiped God, the Creator, instead of the things He has created."

"We have a lot of work yet to do," said Lois.

# Chapter 6

# A-E-I-O

Lois looked out the window of the school kitchen. *That looks like Tom Harvey's pickup*, she thought. *I wonder what he wants?*

Just then Betty Harvey, one of the school girls, came into the kitchen. "My Daddy wants to be a Christian!" she said.

"Invite him in," Lois replied. She rushed to find Vern.

"He's already gone," said one of the boys.

"Is our Navajo pastor still here?" Lois asked.

"No!"

Lois prayed all the way into the other room. *Lord, it's up to me to guide Tom to find You as his Savior. Please help me.*

She sat down with Tom and Betty. For the next two and one-half hours she explained how Tom could become a Christian. Betty interpreted into the Navajo language.

Then Tom said softly, "I want to pray now."

Lois turned to Betty and said, "This would be a good time for you to give your life to the Lord, also."

They all prayed. Then they talked and prayed again.

"You are both new Christians," said Lois as she smiled.

A few weeks later, Nanabah, Tom's wife, told the missionaries, "I'm ready to accept the Lord now. I want to live for Jesus like my husband and daughter."

"It takes courage and determination for the Navajos to give up their old ceremonies and beliefs," Vern said to Lois. "Some of them have lots of persecution in their home camps. Family members try to convince them to give up their new Christian life."

Later they were excited to hear Nanabah say, "We are determined to live for the Lord. My mother, however, made us move away from our family camp. We wouldn't participate in the medicine man's ceremonies when she was sick. But we won't be defeated!"

"Praise the Lord!" said Vern. Everyone praised the Lord when Nanabah's mother became a Christian a few months after that.

\* \* \*

One spring morning Vern said to Lois, "We need to go up to the mesa on Black Mountain and visit some of our Christians there."

*Mary Gafford, teacher, with the children of the Rough Rock Mission School*

Shady places on the narrow road were still shiny with ice and snow. Spots of thick black mud appeared where the sun reached the ground. Vern and Lois slowly made their way along the treacherous road. He laughingly said, "It's a good driver who can hit all the holes in this road!"

Lois looked down at the sharp edge of the road and the valley far below. "And there's no place to dodge the bumps," she replied.

They stopped at the first camp to visit a Christian woman. "She isn't here," said her daughter-in-law. "She's out herding the sheep."

They visited with the young woman awhile. They sang some hymns and read Scripture. Vern explained the meaning of the verses.

"Do you know Jesus as your personal Savior?" Lois asked.

Tears came to the young woman's eyes. "No, but I'd like to be saved."

"We could pray right now."

They knelt together. The young Navajo mother asked God to forgive her. After they finished praying, Vern and Lois told the young woman, "We'll go on to visit others, now. We will pray for you every day."

This time Vern put chains on the wheels of their vehicle. "These roads are too slick without them," he said.

Soon they came to the older woman and her flock of sheep. "We're glad that your daughter-in-law is a Christian now," Lois said.

Vern had prayer with her. As they started to leave, he said, "We'll ask God to help you continue to be faithful to Him."

By that time the washes ran full of melting snow. "We'll have to save the rest of our visiting until the roads get better," Vern said, turning back down the mountain.

* * *

The missionaries began to plan special classes for adults. Sometime later the Adult Bible Schools came into being. Some sessions took place at

Rough Rock. Others were on the mountain at Oak Ridge. Each school included Bible study classes, a worship class, and reading classes. The attenders also memorized many Scripture verses.

"It's important for us to teach them how to read their Bibles," said Lois. "People have a hard time being Christians if they can't read the Bible in their own language."

First she explained the Navajo vowel sounds— a,e,i,o. Then she sounded out the consonants. Lois showed how vowels and consonants formed syllables. "Syllables become words," she explained.

She printed the Navajo version of "I can do all things through Christ which strengtheneth me" (Philippians 4:13), on the chalkboard. *Christ sidziilgo 'asosinii bee t'aa'altsoni 'adeeshliilgo bineesh'a.* All eyes followed the pointer as she helped the adults repeat the sounds.

"This is what we've been waiting for," they exclaimed. Their faces shone with new joy.

These thirty- or forty- or fifty-year-olds worked hard to come to Bible School. Some couldn't stay for the whole four weeks. Sometimes the wife and her little children came for the first two weeks. Her husband stayed home to take care of the sheep. Then he came the final two weeks while she stayed home.

\* \* \*

In 1963 a friend from Iowa bought a four-wheel-drive carryall for the mission.

"This is a gift from the Lord," said Vern. "It will help us get to places we couldn't go otherwise."

One day a hard rainstorm came up as they visited on the mesa. On the way back down to Rough Rock they came to a deep wash.

"This still looks dry, like it is most of the time," said Vern. He started to drive across.

All at once Lois looked to the right. "Vern!" she yelled. "There's a huge wall of water coming down the wash!"

Logs rolled ahead of the water as it raced toward the white carryall.

*The white carryall stuck in a muddy wash on Black Mesa*

## Chapter 7

# EIGHT DEAD GOATS

Vern tried to make the carryall go faster! Just then the water and logs slammed against the vehicle. "We're stuck!" he said.

"The water's getting higher," said Lois.

Vern shifted into four-wheel-drive. The carryall shuddered, then lunged ahead onto firm ground. "If we hadn't had this four-wheel-drive, we would have been washed downstream with the logs and water," he said.

\* \* \*

The vehicle worked well for taking people to camp meeting up on the mountain at Oak Ridge. "Let's stay for the evening service," someone suggested. Lois, the driver, thought, *I don't know what the roads will be like after this rain, but I've got the four-wheel-drive.*

After the service they started down to Rough Rock. Just below Oak Ridge they came to a pickup stuck in the middle of a big wash.

"Can we help you?" Lois yelled out the window.

"Yes," a man replied. "But you'd better put chains on first. It's really slick out here." Several men helped put the chains on the carryall wheels.

"The pickup's tipped a lot to one side," said one of the Navajo men as he looked over the situation again.

"You'd better not try to pull it out, especially in the dark," advised another.

"We can take you on home, then," said Lois. People from the pickup crowded into the carryall. The fast-flowing water splashed vigorously as she drove safely across. A few miles on down the road they came to another pickup.

"It's stuck in a muddy rut," Lois said.

Several people rushed to meet the carryall. "Can we go with you?" they asked eagerly.

Lois looked at the load in the back of the carryall. "I don't see how we can take any more," she said.

"But we've got several children with us," pleaded one woman who shivered in the cold dampness.

A voice behind Lois called out, "Sure! We'll move over!"

By the time everyone jammed in out of the rain, Lois counted 19 people. "We're sure glad you came along just when you did," they said.

\* \* \*

Amos and Marie Redhair stayed true to their promise to live for God. One year they announced,

"We want a camp meeting this summer at our family camp." Amos set the date for the last week of July.

Vern and Lois gladly helped them make plans. "It'll be a good time of fellowship for the Navajos who live up there," they said. "There'll be good food and many spiritual blessings, too, just like the other camp meetings we've had each year."

The Redhair camp meeting began on Friday night, as did all the others. From then until Sunday afternoon the people had services together. They took time out only for meals and a few hours of sleep at night.

Before every service the women set the large kettles of mutton stew on the open fire. Then, an hour before the service ended, several ladies hurried out to work the fry bread dough into thin, round patties. Just before time to eat, they fried the patties in hot fat.

The Navajos chatted happily as they waited in the long line for the delicious stew and fry bread. As soon as they finished eating the ladies pitched in to help with the cleanup. No one wanted to miss the beginning of the next service.

Vern had a surprise when he arrived one day at the Redhair camp meeting. He saw a certain man sitting up in front. *He's never had anything to do with the Gospel before*, Vern thought.

This man stood to speak at the close of the service. "I didn't want the church up here. In fact, I always said I didn't need the Christians. Now I need them! Two days ago lightning killed eight of my goats. Of course none of my family or I can touch them. But I don't think the Christians are afraid to haul the goats off and bury them."

"I'll bury the goats," said Vern.

"I'll go, too," said Amos. Another Navajo Christian man agreed to help as well. After dinner the men took Amos's pickup and loaded the dead goats into the back.

"Take everything that's all around there under the trees," shouted the man's family from a distance. The men untied the clothes line with its load of clothespins. They grabbed up the buckets and the cans, too. They hauled everything off to a spot a mile away. There they dug a hole big enough to bury the goats and all. Sometime after that, the man, his wife, and their son became Christians.

\* \* \*

Later that year Vern began to feel sick. Soon the doctor said, "You must go away for a complete rest."

The Ellis family prayed about the matter. They talked it over. Before long they sadly agreed to take the doctor's advice.

"We will miss you," said the Navajos who had a going-away party for Vern and Lois. The Ellises were gone from Rough Rock for several months. During that time other missionaries came to help at the mission.

Vern had an operation. After that he slowly began to feel better. The doctor examined him again. "I think you are well enough to go back to your mission work," he said.

As soon as they returned Vern and Lois found themselves as busy as ever. Mary Gafford stayed on to help, even though the mission school did not open that year.

One day the three of them drove to the town called Many Farms to do their usual errands. "It doesn't matter that it's raining. We've got the four-wheel-drive," said Vern.

They picked up their mail as well as some for the government school and Trading Post. After they finished their shopping they started back to Rough Rock.

"I believe it's rained all day," said Lois.

"I'm glad Vern knows how to drive through the washes. They're sure to be running high with water," said Mary from the back seat.

Before long they came to just such a wash. Vern drove most of the way across. Suddenly the carryall dropped into a hole.

He tried to back up. "We're in clear up to the hub caps!" he said. Every time the wheels moved they sank deeper. "The mud's like quicksand. We'll just wait a bit. It isn't raining now. It looks to me like the water's going down."

They waited for several minutes. Vern tried once again to go forward. Nothing happened. He tried to force the carryall to go backward. It only settled deeper.

"There's no solid ground here!" he muttered.

Just then a woman and her daughter hurried into sight. "We live half a mile from here," she explained, "and we know it's raining up above. We must get you out. More water is sure to be here soon."

The two of them started using their shovels. Vern shoveled fast, too. They worked and worked. It got dark. Still they couldn't get the carryall to move. The water began coming up. Finally Vern said, "We've done everything we can think of. There's no way we can get out of this wash without help."

He looked at his watch. "It's eleven o'clock. You ladies had better go on home. We sure do appreciate your help, though." The Navajo woman and her daughter turned toward their house. Vern said goodbye to Lois and Mary and began walking back to Many Farms.

The missionary women climbed back into the carryall. Their hair and clothes dripped water. They shivered. Soon the water rose higher in the wash. It seeped onto the floor of the carryall. Lois lifted the sacks of mail onto the back seat. "Let's put our feet up on the seat so they won't get any wetter," she suggested.

After a while they shared a box of special crackers Mary had bought at the store. Then Lois remembered a package in the mail sack. "I imagine it has baby blankets in it," she said. "Let's see!"

They opened the package. "Just as I thought," Lois said. "Here, let's each take a little blanket to put over our shoulders."

"That'll at least keep us a bit warmer," Mary agreed.

As daylight began to creep onto the reservation, Lois spotted headlights coming their way. "Vern's here with a wrecker!" she exclaimed.

Before long the wrecker succeeded in pulling the carryall out of the mud.

\* \* \*

"God, please send us the children You want in our daily vacation Bible school this summer," Lois prayed as she knocked on the hogan door.

Shy brown faces peeked out at her. "I'm here to pick up girls for our Bible school this week," she explained. "They can come and stay at the mission. We'll bring them home at the end of the week and pick up the boys for next week's session."

Soon the carryall had a full load of wiggling, giggling girls. When they arrived at the mission they sat down to dinner. Each one had a turn in the shower before going to bed.

"The girls surely do enjoy the good warm water," said Lois. "Water has to be used sparingly in their homes. Most of the families haul their water in from a long distance."

The girls enjoyed every minute of the playground fun, songs, and Bible stories. Visiting workers helped them study their Bibles and learn Scripture verses. Everyone had opportunity to make something special during the handcraft sessions.

The week soon passed. It came time to take the girls back home to herd sheep and to help care for younger brothers and sisters.

The boys came the next week. They liked everything just as much as the girls did.

\* \* \*

"It's good to be back in the house where it's warm and dry," said Vern at ten o'clock one New Year's Eve.

"I'm glad, though, you could use the carryall to help pull some of the pickups out of the snowdrifts," said Lois as she poured hot coffee into a big mug.

"The roads are completely blocked with snowdrifts now," Vern said, stretching his feet toward the warm stove.

All at once he heard a knock at the door.

"Can you come help us?" a man pleaded.

## Chapter 8

# THE APPRECIATION PARTY

Vern looked past the man who stood in the open doorway. The snowstorm had let up. Moonlight reflected off the white reservation. "What can I do for you?" he asked.

"There are 17 vehicles out there, all stuck in snowbanks. Can you bring the government bulldozer to get the cars out? Two families have sick babies they need to take to the doctor."

"The bulldozer doesn't have lights," Vern replied. "I don't see how I can use it, but we'll have to do something." He stepped outside in the clear, cold air.

"I believe the moonlight is bright enough to see by," he said.

Vern quickly cranked the bulldozer motor and chugged out to the road. Snow sprayed high and wide from in front of the big blade. It moved the great piles of snow away from first one vehicle, then another.

Navajos often asked Vern to drive the big bulldozer, owned by the Bureau of Indian Affairs. He used it to widen the road up Black Mountain. One man said, "Reverend Ellis has been out there every day. He works so long and hard that it almost embarrasses the others to quit for the day. He's really been great!"

Later a man from Colorado gave a bulldozer to the mission. "This is going to be a big help," said Vern. Sometimes he worked on the roads. He used the bulldozer to build ponds so the Navajos could have more water for their sheep and cattle. Some asked him to level the ground for new cabins. He gladly helped them whether they could pay the cost of the gas or not.

Vern used all of these opportunities to tell the people about what God could do for them. Once he and a Navajo man sat on the ground in front of the bulldozer to study the Bible.

\* \* \*

Through the years many people came to help Vern and Lois at Rough Rock. "You are a real help to us," they said. "There's always so much to do and not nearly enough time to get it all done."

One summer a group of young people came from Newberg, Oregon. They worked hard to put a new culvert under the road. A downpour of rain washed it out. They put it in again the next day. Another rain washed it out that night. The day before they left, the high schoolers put the culvert

*Vern at work in the mission shop*

back in place. As they drove away the next morning, they saw the rain had washed their culvert out for the third time.

Lois waved as the bus pulled away. *We pray they will want to obey God wherever He calls them,* she thought. She had no idea that one of those young men would someday come back to Rough Rock as a missionary.

Another group planned to arrive on a certain Saturday. Vern and Lois had been gone all week to Adult Bible School on the mountain.

"What's that horrible smell?" Lois asked as they walked into their house Friday afternoon.

Vern sniffed! "It's the refrigerator! It quit working!"

All the food had spoiled. They thought about how much it would cost to buy a new refrigerator. "What will we do?" Lois wanted to know. "How can I keep food fresh for the group without the fridge?"

They cleaned up the smelly mess. Afterward they sat down to look through their mail. "Here's a check," said Vern. "The letter with it says, 'Use this wherever it's needed!'"

He held the check where Lois could see it. "$275!" she exclaimed. "Why, that's just the amount we need to buy a new refrigerator!"

"Isn't God good!" said Vern. "He knew what we needed before we knew it ourselves."

One winter Vern and Lois prayed for enough money to buy groceries for the schoolchildren. A lady from the Oak Ridge area came to see them. Lois served coffee and also gave the visitor something to eat. Pretty soon the woman handed Vern a tiny roll of paper tied with bright gift ribbon. He took the ribbon off and unrolled the paper. On it were the words, "This I give you." A small drawing of a calf filled the rest of the space.

Tears came to Vern's eyes. "Look at this, Lois. She's giving us a calf so we'll have meat for the schoolchildren." He turned to the woman and said, "Thank you!"

"What a wonderful answer to our prayers," Lois added.

\* \* \*

"At last! We can relax this evening," Lois told Vern that Friday. "This has been such a busy day."

Then came a loud knock. The door flung open, and an eight-year-old girl popped in. Lois recognized her.

She quickly drew the shivering girl close to the stove. Lois picked up a towel and dried the girl's hands, which were blue with cold. "Here, sit by the stove." Lois hurried to make hot cocoa. She set a plate of oatmeal cookies on the table close by.

"Tell us what happened," she said gently.

"My Daddy and Mother are drinking. I ran away when they started fighting!" The girl eagerly gulped the cocoa. "I slid down the trail 'cuz it's so icy. My parents yelled at me to come back. But I hollered at them and said, 'No! I'm going to the mission! I'm going to see Vern and Lois. They love me over there!' "

Bright headlights shone through the window. The frightened girl whirled and dashed into the dark bedroom. She hid behind the bed.

Her parents came to the front door. "Is our girl here?" they asked. "We've come to take her home!"

"She's here, but she doesn't want to go home tonight," Vern replied firmly.

"You should let her stay until tomorrow," said Lois. "You can come for her in the morning."

After more conversation the parents agreed to the suggestion and went on home. The little girl came out of her hiding place.

Lois made a bed on the couch. She and Vern prayed with their guest. "Dear Jesus, please help her parents come to know You." After that she slept soundly all night.

The next morning the girl woke up happy. She folded the blankets neatly and ate a good breakfast. Her mother and father came for her in the middle of the morning. She obediently went home with them.

\* \* \*

"It hardly seems possible we've been here at Rough Rock for twenty years," said Lois.

"We want to have an appreciation party for you," said the Navajos. "Others have come and gone, but you've stayed."

The day of the party started off cloudy and foggy, but not cold. The celebration got underway in the Rough Rock church at eleven o'clock. A young man who had grown up there had charge of the service. He spoke appreciation for Vern and Lois in both English and Navajo. After that a guest speaker preached a message.

Several of the Christians came to the platform and sang songs in their language. The speaker and his wife also sang a special number in Navajo.

Little children cried or talked aloud. Doors banged as people went in and out. Vern and Lois sat quietly. *These are our precious brothers and sisters in the Lord*, they thought.

"Vern and Lois," said the young man, "we want you to come forward now to receive the gifts we have brought. You deserve a lot more, but this is the best we can do."

*It looks like a mountain of presents there in the corner of the platform*, thought Lois. They opened the gifts one by one: handmade silver and turquoise jewelry as well as colorful handwoven rugs and blankets.

"Thank you for the way you've remembered us today," said Lois. "Thank you, also, for loving our children as they grew up. Thank you for your prayers. You mean so much to us."

Vern also thanked the people for the gifts. "God gets the credit for any good we've been able to do," he added.

Navajos expressed their appreciation to the Ellises. "You've helped to improve our roads. You've helped a lot of us learn to read. Many of us are well because you took us to the doctor and hospital."

Vern named others who had helped at the mission. "A lot of people have helped, not just us. Do you know what brings the greatest joy and happiness to Lois and me? It's knowing that many of you have accepted the Lord and are living for Jesus. We encourage those of you who aren't yet Christians to accept Jesus as your Savior."

At two o'clock everyone walked over to the school cafeteria. Together they enjoyed the roast ribs, stew, salad, fry bread, pie, and peaches.

That night at home Vern and Lois talked about the wonderful appreciation party. "I hope people will continue to pray for us," said Vern.

"Yes," Lois agreed. "We'll need God's help in the years ahead."

*The airplane transported passengers as well as freight. Boys in Bible class at the Rough Rock Elementary School*

# Chapter 9

# NAME THAT TUNE!

"Heavy snows and rain caused an emergency near the Rough Rock Friends Mission in Arizona," said the article in the newspaper.

Vern and Lois lived in the middle of that emergency in February 1978. They watched as the melting snow changed the dirt roads into deep muddy streams. Then the rain started and travel became impossible.

Schools were closed. Neighbors couldn't get around to help each other. Fresh water supplies weren't fit to use. Livestock either died or waited helplessly without food or water.

Vern became a member of the "emergency committee." He pointed to the map. "Here are many family camps that are stranded up there on the mesa," he said. "I can show you where they live. They all need our help!"

The committee made a plan. "We'll get big National Guard helicopters to airlift supplies in," they decided.

Many people helped fill special bags with emergency food. They unloaded hay from big trucks. Then the helicopters arrived. Men filled them with the two thousand bales of hay, as well as food, water, and other supplies. Vern and Lois worked alongside everyone else.

The emergency continued over Sunday. Vern rushed to the airstrip to make sure more hay and food were available. Early that morning Lois saw that their living room overflowed with Indians waiting for the weather to clear. She quickly baked enough coffee cake for seventy people before she and Mary Gafford drove the bus to gather the children for Sunday school. Later they told Vern, "We had 45 – the most we've had all year on Sunday morning!"

\* \* \*

One day the phone rang. Lois recognized the voice at the other end. *She was one of the girls in our first high school Bible class at Many Farms*, she thought.

"Lois, what was the song we used to sing about living close to Jesus?" the voice asked. "We sang it a lot in your Bible class at Many Farms."

Lois thought of all the songs the high schoolers had enjoyed. The voice went on. "I'm married now and live in another town. I'm going to give my testimony in church next Sunday. I want to use the words of that song, but I can't remember how it goes."

"I can't think what song you mean," Lois answered.

"The tune goes like this." The young woman began to hum.

"Oh, now I know!" Lois exclaimed. " 'Just a Closer Walk with Thee.' That's the one! We used to sing it nearly every class time. I'll be glad to send you a copy of the words."

Vern and Lois drove to Many Farms every week to lead the Bible class at the high school. In the middle of one year a new superintendent arrived to take charge of the school.

When the Ellises went to class a few weeks later they discovered this message: "Go to the office!"

The secretary immediately said to Lois, "I'll tell the superintendent you're here!"

Soon a large man bustled in and said gruffly, "I saw that poster about your Bible class. How long have you been having Bible class here?"

Lois replied gently, "Well, probably about 15 years—since the school first started here at Many Farms. The principal gave us permission. Why? Has there been some complaint?"

"No! There's been no complaint. If there had been, I would have known what was going on."

The superintendent paced the floor in front of Lois. "After this, everyone who attends your class must have a permission slip signed by his or her parents. Besides that, every week I want a list of the students who came that day."

Lois looked him directly in the eye. "I can do that, even though we have 45 or 50 who come each week. I'll be glad to get permission slips. Do you want me to make my own or will you furnish them?"

"I'll furnish them!" he replied crossly. "That'll be all for now."

Lois hurried back to the classroom. "I'm afraid we won't be allowed to have Bible class here anymore after this year," she told Vern.

The next week Lois explained to the students, "You'll need to take these permission slips home. Your parents must sign them so you can come to our class."

The week following she returned the signed forms to the office. Every week after that, the students signed the list that went to the superintendent.

On the last day of school that year Lois said sadly, "I don't suppose we'll be able to have any more Bible classes here."

"That's too bad," Vern replied. "We enjoy this work so much."

Two weeks later they received a letter from the superintendent. *I'm almost afraid to open this*, Lois thought. The letter said, "We think it's great for you to have Bible classes here. We want you to come back next fall. There will be a room ready for you."

*Lois with Helen Deschenie, having Bible study at a Navajo home*

Lois smiled and put the letter back into the envelope. "This is another answer to prayer!" she said.

\* \* \*

Lois enjoyed doing camp visitation. Sometimes she and one of the Navajo women, Helen Deschenie, spent a whole day together going from camp to camp.

"Let's go toward Sam and Sandra's home," Lois suggested at the beginning of one visitation day.

They saw the couple and their two little boys walking toward the highway. "We're on our way to catch a ride to Many Farms," Sam told them. "We don't have a pickup of our own anymore since I don't have a job."

"We left the baby with Sam's mother," Sandra said.

"Come on with us," Lois invited. "We'll take you as far as the next turnoff."

On the way, Sam and Sandra told about some of their problems and disappointments. Lois said, "Let me pray for you." She asked God to help this young family.

She and Helen drove on to the next home. The two ladies who lived there had lots of work to do. One of them bent over a pan filled with dirty dishes. Her sister knelt down to feed lambs from a bottle. They both gladly put their work aside to visit and to listen as Helen read some Bible verses. They all prayed together before Lois and Helen went on their way.

The woman at the next cabin waved to them from the sheep corral. As soon as she finished caring for the lambs and baby goats she climbed into the pickup with Lois and Helen.

"My husband works in Farmington," she said. "He's home only on weekends. I have all the work here to do by myself during the week. He won't let me go to church, either. I'm sure God has some help for me, though."

"Yes, He does," Lois assured her. She read Scripture verses and then led in prayer.

"It's time for me to turn my sheep out now," the Navajo woman said. "I'll spend the day herding them."

They stopped to see Kathryn and Wayne. After lunch they drove on to see Mary and Irene at their homes. Next they visited with a man patching holes in the fence around his sheep corral. "My wife is out hunting a lost sheep," he told them.

As they drove away they met the woman coming back. "Did you find your sheep?" they asked.

"No!" she said, looking worried and tired.

Lois and Helen went on to have a service with John and his grown son Leon. They had fun talking about the good times they had enjoyed when Leon attended school at the mission.

On their way back to Rough Rock the women prayed, "Bless and help those who heard Your Word today!"

\* \* \*

One day in 1985 more missionaries came to Rough Rock Friends Mission. Vern and Lois introduced them to the Navajos. "This is Bob Hampton and his wife Cheri and their little boy named Justin."

Vern made sure Bob saw the culvert.

"I see it finally stayed in!" Bob said with a hearty laugh.

"Yes, but you young people from Newberg did work hard! We felt sorry the rain washed it out so many times!"

Vern and Lois helped the Hamptons get settled. "We remember what it's like to be the new missionaries," they said, "and we want to help you in every way we can."

The two families worked together for the next few months.

Keith and his Navajo friend, Kee;
Patricia, Eva, Joyce, and Sandra riding their friends' horses

# Chapter 10

# REMEMBER WHEN?

"We've lived here on the Navajo reservation almost thirty years," said Vern one day.

"My, what a lot of changes we've seen!" Lois replied. "Changes here on the reservation, and in our family, too. Our children are all grown up now and married, with children of their own."

"Aren't we glad they all like to come to Rough Rock and help us when they can!" said Vern.

They talked about the years Keith and his wife, Elizabeth, and their children had been missionaries at Rough Rock. They remembered visits from their other children and grandchildren.

They talked about the changes on the reservation. More jobs were available for the Indians. Many of them could buy cars and pickups to replace the teams of horses and wagons.

"The women drive the cars and pickups just as well as the men do," Lois said.

"Now the Navajos haul their water barrels in the back of their pickups," Vern observed. "It doesn't take near as long as it used to with their wagons."

As the Navajos built new, larger homes, some of their hogans disappeared. People lived longer because they could more easily get medical help.

"Even so, some must travel one hundred miles to a doctor," said Lois. "With all the changes, though, the women still wear their pleated skirts and bright colored velveteen blouses for special occasions. They've kept on weaving their beautiful rugs, too."

"The men continue to use silver and turquoise to make the valuable jewelry and belts," said Vern.

"Selling their handmade things is one way Navajos can earn more money," reminded Lois.

"Men's clothes have changed some," Vern noted. "We see more western-style clothes on the reservation than we used to. And don't forget, nowadays some of the camps have television as well as electricity. Maybe sometime there'll be enough jobs for all who want to work."

"But one thing hasn't changed!" Lois said. "They still need the Lord!" Later she wrote in a letter, "We minister to people who are seeing many changes now, with more changes coming. We're glad we can tell them about Jesus, who is the same yesterday, today, and forever!"

Someone who knew Vern and Lois well said, "The Ellises have not changed over these thirty years. They have been consistent in their Christian example. They've always loved the Navajos and have faithfully presented the Gospel to them."

Then the time came for the Ellises to retire.

The Rough Rock community and the government school sponsored a special dinner in the Rough Rock school cafeteria on December 18, 1985. "We want to honor our long-time missionaries," they said.

Three hundred Navajos came to watch Vern and Lois receive a beautiful Navajo rug and a letter of commendation from the Navajo Tribal Chairman, Paterson Zah. Part of the letter said, "You have made yourself available for round-the-clock service. Your Bible studies and love have influenced so many adults and students. These are your greatest gifts to our people."

"We cherish these wonderful missionaries..." someone said.

Another Navajo stood to say, "We also remember how the Ellises always helped us when our people had disasters."

Vern and Lois held their final service as missionaries at Rough Rock on Sunday, May 25, 1986. The service had been announced for one o'clock in the afternoon, but people began coming before ten o'clock that morning. The Oak Ridge and Red Ridge churches had dismissed their usual services so all could come down the mountain to the mission. The Indian women started early to prepare the food out behind the church where the big grill and the tables were located.

Two singing groups brought the music for the service. A guest speaker preached, urging the Navajos to stay true to the Lord. "You must take responsibility for God's work here," he said.

Many of the Indians spoke their appreciation for Vern and Lois. "Please come up here in front," the speaker said. As the Ellises stood on the platform, about three hundred Indians came to give them big hugs. "We'll miss you," the Navajos said as tears ran down their faces.

After the service everyone went outside. The tables were loaded with rugs, jewelry, blankets, clocks, plaques, pottery, folding chairs, an electric lantern, and money. Vern and Lois felt humble as they opened these gifts.

Then came the meal. Everyone had all the stew, fry bread, salads, and watermelon they could eat. "We didn't know so many cared so much," said Vern and Lois. "How we love these people!"

They finished packing their household items. Vern took part in the graduation exercises that Wednesday. "We will be leaving early tomorrow morning," he told the Indians gathered for the occasion. "This will be our final good-bye to you."

No one wanted to miss the chance to tell their missionaries good-bye. People kept coming to the mission house until after eleven o'clock that night. More came for a last farewell early on Thursday morning. Several stayed to wave as Vern and Lois drove out of the mission yard. Some who lived close to the road came out to wave as the Ellises passed by. "It's hard to leave them all," Vern said. They took one last look at Black Mountain.

"So many of our friends live up there on the mesa," said Lois.

"The roads are a lot better than when we came," Vern replied. "Irene and Mary and John and the others can get down here easier than in the early years."

"They will probably always get snowed in during hard storms in the winter, though," Lois said.

The main road, paved now, stretched out before them. *We'll always remember the many times we were stuck in the mud or sand along here,* they thought.

Their lives would be different from now on, but one thing would be the same: "We'll still love the Navajos!" they said.

\* \* \*

A few weeks later in Colorado many Friends from the Rocky Mountain area gathered for a special service. After the first hymn a man stepped behind the pulpit and announced, "Vern and Lois Ellis, we want you to come forward. *This is your life!*"

Vern and Lois looked at one another in surprise. They slowly walked to the platform. Merle Roe, the man behind the pulpit, pointed to two chairs nearby. The Ellises sat down. Friends and family members began to tell of their love and appreciation for Vern and Lois.

"I feel it was a real privilege to work with Vern and Lois all those years," said Mary Gafford.

Pastor Joe Hodges said, "They always wanted to do the will of God."

Others recalled the years Vern and Lois pastored the Friends church at Springbank. Their son, Keith, told about things he remembered. Merle Roe read a kind letter from Vern and Lois's daughter Sandra.

Vern and Lois laughed as speakers told some of the funny things that had happened through the years. They wiped tears from their eyes as people talked about blessings and answers to prayer.

Toward the end of the service the president of the Mission Board handed a new Bible to Vern and one to Lois. He also gave them a check. "This money shows our love. God bless you!" he said.

Vern and Lois hardly knew what to say. Slowly, Lois stepped to the pulpit.

Tearfully she said, "Thank you for the Bibles and for the money." She dabbed at her eyes and added, "Thank you for your love and prayers. Without your prayers we couldn't have done what God wanted us to do. Please continue to pray for us."

Vern wiped his eyes as he stood beside Lois. "Anything we've done over the years is to the Lord's credit, not ours," he said. "We thank you from the bottom of our hearts."

\* \* \*

Vern and Lois visited each of their children for the next few months. In 1987 people from the

Friends church in Penrose, Colorado, asked, "Will you come to be our pastors?"

They prayed about this invitation. In a short while they sent their reply. "Yes, we feel that God wants us to go to Penrose."

One day soon after that they had a phone call. When Lois finished answering the phone she said to Vern, "There's going to be a book written about our life at Rough Rock. We must look through our letters and other papers to find information for the book."

"We can think about that while we get settled into the parsonage at Penrose," Vern replied.

They looked at letters and pictures and articles they had written. It all brought back memories.

"Look, Vern, here's a picture of a Christmas program." Lois smiled and added, "Remember when I mixed up 22 batches of refrigerator dough? They made up into 618 sweet rolls for the community Christmas service."

Vern did remember. "You really had a reputation as a good cook. Those cinnamon rolls you made for Bible studies and other events went over well. I've also heard a lot of people say your Indian fry bread is as good as the Navajos make."

Another day Lois found a picture of the children who attended the first daily vacation Bible school. "That was our first year at Rough Rock," she said.

Vern looked at the picture. "Those children are all adults now. Isn't it amazing that even after all these years, a lot of them have the pictures they made that week still hanging on their walls!"

They talked about how important the camp meetings had been in the lives of the Christians. "What wonderful days those were," Vern said.

"Look, here's a report we wrote in 1965," said Lois. "Seventy-three doctor trips to the clinic at Chinle and 19 trips to the hospital at Ganado."

"Let's see, how many miles is that?" Vern wondered. "Seventy-three trips times 35 miles each way—that equals 5,110 miles. Nineteen trips times 70 miles each way—that's 2,660 miles."

"That was just one year," Lois said, "and only the doctor trips. It doesn't count the miles we traveled across the reservation to help in other ways, or to visit or have camp meetings or Bible school up on Black Mountain, or to take people home or go get them for something. How many miles did we travel in the thirty years we were there?"

"A lot!" Vern replied.

"We prayed on every trip, *Lord, help us teach the Bible truths in a way that is simple enough to be understood and yet challenging.* That was our goal for everything we did." Lois finished tying the bundle of papers.

"There are sure lots of memories in that package," said Vern.

"While you take it to the post office, I'll mix up a batch of dough for cinnamon rolls," Lois said. "Someone may come for help today, and I'll want to have something warm to serve with the coffee."